Sensational Hot Pot Recipes

A Fantastic Cookbook of Tasty Asian Dish Ideas!

Table of Contents

Introduction 4

   1 – Hot Pot Dipping Sauces 6

   Teriyaki Sauce 7

   Garlic Sauce 8

   Sesame Sauce 9

   Ponzu Sauce 10

   2 – Mushroom Ginger Hot Pot 11

   3 – Vegan Chinese Hot Pot 14

   4 – Bacon-Clam Hot Pot 17

   5 – Japanese Shiitake Salmon Hot Pot 20

   6 – Sukiyaki Hot Pot 22

   7 – Potato Lamb Hot Pot 25

   8 – Seafood Noodle Hot Pot 27

   9 – Tofu Mushroom Hot Pot 30

   10 – Beef Mince Hot Pot 33

   11 – Vietnamese Hot Pot 36

   12 – Onion Potato Hot Pot 39

   13 – Sausage Lentil Hot Pot 41

   14 – Pumpkin Udon Hot Pot 44

   15 – Green Bean Ginger Hot Pot 47

   16 – Lancashire Potato Hot Pot 50

   17 – Spicy Lo Mein Tofu Hot Pot 53

18 – Pork Mushroom Hot Pot 56
19 – Thai Chicken Hot Pot..58
20 – Chinese Mung Bean Hot Pot...61
21 – Bavarian Hot Pot..63
22 – Asian Beef Mushroom Hot Pot 66
23 – Korean Dumpling Hot Pot 69
24 – Miso Noodle Hot Pot 71
25 – Mongolian Chinese Hot Pot...74
26 – Sukiyaki Vegan Hot Pot 76
27 – Pork Ribs Hot Pot..79
28 – Vegetable Beef Japanese Hot Pot 81
29 – Spicy Whitefish Hot Pot 84
30 – Thai Curry Coconut Hot Pot 86

Conclusion 88

Introduction

How can you integrate hot pot foods into your recipe repertoire at home?

Can you seek out the different varieties of ingredients you'll need to make these dishes?

Are you curious about the various ways in which hot pots can make your recipes tastier?

Above all, have fun when you serve hot pot dinners. It's an experience that you can share with others, and enjoy their company while you're eating. Experiment with hot pots and discover your personal preferences, and have fun while you learn.

In this cookbook, you'll discover how to use a hot pot in 30 different dishes.

Read on and try out some of these tasty recipes. You may even find more dishes that can benefit from the inclusion of a pleasant get-together with friends.

1 – Hot Pot Dipping Sauces

Many hot pot recipes are set up for the meat, tofu and/or vegetables to be cooked at a communal table. Some are less traditional, and feature soups and broths that are ladled into individual bowls, even though the meat and vegetables are already cooked. Dipping sauces can be used for either type.

These are the most commonly used dipping sauces for hot pot meals. They are easy to make, and they create a wonderful taste sensation when combined with the freshly cooked meats and vegetables.

Teriyaki Sauce

Ingredients

- 4 to 5 tbsp. honey, pure
- 1 tbsp. corn starch
- 1/2 cup water, filtered
- 1/4 cup soy sauce, reduced sodium

Garlic Sauce

Ingredients

- 1/4 cup oil, canola
- 1 tsp. salt, kosher
- 1/4 cup lemon juice, fresh
- 1/4 cup garlic, minced

Sesame Sauce

Ingredients

- 2 cups water, purified
- 1/2 cup soy sauce (shoyu), low sodium
- 1/3 cup Tahini
- 1 tbsp. mustard
- 1/4 cup sake
- 1/2 cup vinegar, rice
- 1/3 cup mirin
- 1/4 cup sugar, granulated
- 1/4 cup miso
- 1/3 cup ground sesame seeds, toasted

Ponzu Sauce

Ingredients

- 1/2 tsp. of fresh ginger, grated
- 1 1/2 cups of water, filtered
- 1/4 cup vinegar
- 1/2 cup soy sauce (shoyu), low sodium
- 1/2 cup lemon juice, fresh

2 – Mushroom Ginger Hot Pot

Sometimes, flavors just seem to possess you. Today I was planning on a plain bowl of soup for lunch, but then I saw other veggies at the store and wanted to try them out. Mushroom and ginger go together so well, especially on chilly days.

Makes 2-4 Servings

Cooking + Prep Time: 1 hour 10 minutes

Ingredients:

- 1 x 15-ounce can of coconut milk, light
- 1 tomato, chopped
- 2 tbsp. of soy sauce
- 1 ounce of shiitake mushrooms, dried
- ¼ tsp. of cinnamon, ground
- 2 x star anise
- ½ tsp. of pepper flakes, red, crushed
- 1 tbsp. of ginger, minced
- 2 tbsp. of lemon grass, minced
- 3 cloves of minced garlic
- 1 tbsp. of corn starch
- 4 cups of vegetable or mushroom broth
- 1 sliced onion, red
- 1 tbsp. of sesame oil, toasted
- 1 lg. pinch of sea salt, coarse
- 1 sliced bell pepper, red
- ½ lime, juice only
- Black pepper, fresh
- Rice noodles, cooked, to serve
- Dipping sauces, your choice – see recipe 1

Instructions:

1. Heat 4-qt. pot on med. heat. Mix broth and corn starch. Set this aside.

2. Sauté pepper and onion in oil with salt, 'til the onions become soft.

3. Add the pepper flakes, ginger, lemon grass and garlic. Combine well. Cook until the mixture is fragrant. Add and combine corn starch and broth mixture.

4. Add pepper, tomatoes, soy sauce, mushrooms, cinnamon and star anise. Stir for about 10 minutes until broth thickens. Cover hot pot. Bring to boil.

5. Once it boils, reduce to simmer. Cover and cook for about 30 minutes until mushrooms soften completely. Add lime and coconut.

6. Transfer hot pot to heated base on dinner table. Serve to your family and guests with pieces of beef, chicken or tofu and chopsticks, along with dipping sauces.

3 – Vegan Chinese Hot Pot

This is a fun recipe. My friend wanted me to try a vegan meal, and we decided this one would surely fit the bill. This hot pot dish is hearty, and filled with veggies and tofu. They make for a satisfying, filling vegan meal.

Makes 2-4 Servings

Cooking + Prep Time: 8 hours 35 minutes including 8 hours slow cooker time

Ingredients:

For soup

- 60 ounces of stock, vegetable
- 3 tbsp. of soy sauce, low sodium
- ½ tsp. of pepper flakes, red
- 2 tsp. of fish sauce
- 2 tsp. of paste, ginger
- 1 cup of sliced carrots
- 1 chopped onion, medium
- 1 x 8-ounce can of sliced, drained water chestnuts
- 2 tsp. of paste, garlic
- 1 x 8-ounce can of drained bamboo shoots
- 2 sliced sticks of celery

Additions

- 6 chopped green onions
- 1 ounce of 1" cut snow peas, removed strings
- 4 ounces of sliced mushrooms, button
- 8 ounces of drained, cubed tofu, firm
- 2 bunches of sliced baby Bok choy
- Ginger Soy Sauce, bottled

Instructions:

1. Place soup **Ingredients** in slow cooker. Cook for seven to eight hours on a low setting.

2. 20 minutes prior to serving, add "additions", excluding ½ of green onions. Save the other ½ for use as a garnish. Cook for about 20 minutes. Transfer to hot pot on table.

3. Serve spoonful of ginger soy sauce with every soup bowl. Garnish them with reserved ½ of green onions. Allow diners to fill bowls from the hot pot.

4 – Bacon-Clam Hot Pot

This is the hot pot version of clam chowder, with several differences. The broth used is somewhat thinner, and some of the seafood is served whole, so you can really get into it. It is served in a ceramic hot pot, which preserves the wonderful aroma.

Makes 4-6 Servings

Cooking + Prep Time: 1 hour 10 minutes

Ingredients:

- 1 cup of half-and-half
- 1 peeled, diced potato, large
- ½ diced yellow onion, medium
- 2 diced celery stalks
- 3 sliced bacon strips
- 1 tbsp. of oil, olive
- ½ cup miso paste, white or light
- 1 bottle of white wine, dry
- 1 lb. of mussels
- 1 lb. of clams
- 1 sprig of tarragon, fresh
- 1 sprig of rosemary, fresh
- 1 bay leaf
- Kosher salt
- Pepper, white
- Dipping sauces, your choice – see recipe 1

Instructions:

1. Scrub mussels and clams. Rinse well. Discard shells that have opened already.

2. Bring two cups of water and the wine in pot to simmer on med. heat.

3. Add shellfish. Cover. Steam until shells have just opened.

4. Remove shellfish from broth. Discard shells that have not opened. Loosen ½ mussels and clams from shells. Chop them up. Keep other ½ in shells.

5. Strain broth into large sized bowl through sieve. Whisk miso paste into broth 'til it dissolves. Reserve broth with shellfish.

6. In same pot, heat oil on med. heat. Cook onion, bacon and celery until veggies become translucent.

7. Add tarragon, rosemary, bay leaf, reserved broth, potatoes and chopped mussels and clams. Simmer for about 20 minutes. Potatoes should be tender. Season as desired using salt and white pepper.

8. Add whole clams and mussels in shells to half-and-half. Simmer 'til they are heated through. Remove sprigs of herbs. Transfer soup to hot pot. Allow diners to fill their bowls from pot.

5 – Japanese Shiitake Salmon Hot Pot

This weekend I got the chance to cook a dish here that I had previously only had when I dined in Asian restaurants. The Japanese hot pot usually includes meat or fish, with many veggies, all making a flavorful broth.

Makes 2-4 Servings

Cooking + Prep Time: 1/2 hour

Ingredients:

- 2 oz. of shiitake mushrooms, dried
- 1 cup of baby spinach
- 4 cups of stock, vegetable
- 1 cup of carrots, sliced
- white miso
- 1 cup of cabbage
- 6-oz. salmon fillet, boneless
- Dipping sauces, your choice – see recipe 1

Instructions:

1. Prepare the stock in medium pan. Bring to boil.

2. Spread white miso on bottom of your hot pot. Place cabbage, mushrooms, carrots and spinach into pan and pour boiling broth over veggies. Cover with a vented lid.

3. Transfer to hot pot on table. Have your diners use chopsticks or fondue forks to cook the salmon in the hot broth. They can then dip in their choice of sauces.

6 – Sukiyaki Hot Pot

Most people know what sukiyaki is, but fewer have heard of hot pot cuisine. This one-pot wonder has assorted veggies and thin sliced beef, so that your friends and family can cook their own meat in a sweetly simmering broth.

Makes 1-2 Servings

Cooking + Prep Time: 35 minutes

Ingredients:

- 5 or 6 leaves of cabbage, Napa
- 1 chopped scallion stalk
- ½ peeled sliced carrot
- ½ pkg. of sliced tofu, firm
- ½ pkg. of mushrooms, enoki
- ½ lb. of rib eye steak, thin sliced

For broth

- 1 tbsp. of sugar, granulated
- ¼ cup each of filtered water, soy sauce and mirin
- Dipping sauces, your choice – see recipe 1

Instructions:

1. Combine the sugar, water, soy sauce and mirin in sauce pan. Bring to boil. Once boiling, turn heat off. Set the pan aside.

2. Cut steak into very thin slices. Brush loose dirt from mushrooms. Remove and discard roots. Tear them into smaller sized bundles. Set them aside.

3. Slice carrot. Slice tofu in ½" slices. Separate Napa cabbage stem from leaves. Rinse leaves with water. Set them aside.

4. Place all **Ingredients** except steak in hot pot. Pour broth in, as well. Cover. Bring to boil over med-high.

5. Once the pot boils, reduce heat to low and simmer, covered, for an additional 10-15 minutes. Transfer hot pot to dining table.

6. Provide diners with chopsticks to use to cook the thin steak slices.

7 – Potato Lamb Hot Pot

This is such a warming hot pot dish that the entire family will enjoy. Herbs and vegetables make the recipe even more interesting, and everyone is sure to have a wonderful meal.

Makes 3-5 Servings

Cooking + Prep Time: 20 minutes

Ingredients:

- 18-oz. of gravy - beef or lamb
- 1 1/3 pound of lamb, diced
- 1 sliced onion, large
- 1 pound of unpeeled potatoes
- 2 chopped leaves of rosemary sprigs
- Sauces of choice – see recipe 1

Instructions:

1. Slice potatoes to about ¼ of an inch.

2. Heat oven-proof pan on high heat. Tip onion plus most of rosemary into hot pan. Fry for three minutes until onion has softened slightly. Add gravy and stir. Pour soup into hot pot on table. Cook potato slices until they are tender.

3. Provide chopsticks for guests to cook their pieces of lamb.

8 – Seafood Noodle Hot Pot

This is a great recipe to use when you want a relaxed, easy dinner with relatives and friends. You can use the combination of veggies and seafood that appeals to you. You can use up the extra broth over noodles, too, if you like.

Makes 4 servings

Cooking + Prep Time: 40 minutes

Ingredients:

- 1 cup of thawed calamari rings
- 4 halved sea scallops, large
- 12 peeled, de-veined shrimps, large
- ½ cup of straw mushrooms, canned
- 1 or 2 sliced Thai chilies, red
- 2 tbsp. of fish sauce
- 3 tbsp. of vinegar, rice
- 1 cup of coconut milk, light
- 1 x 14-ounce can of tomatoes, diced, with the juice
- 2 ½ cups of stock, chicken
- ½ cup of onion, chopped
- 2 smashed garlic cloves
- 2 sliced shallots
- 1 tbsp. of oil, vegetable
- 4 oz. of noodles, rice stick type, dried
- 2 sprigs of basil
- 6 sprigs of cilantro
- 1 minced stalk of lemon grass
- 1 tbsp. of sugar, granulated
- 2 limes, zest only
- 1 lime, juice only
- Dipping sauces, your choice – see recipe 1

Instructions:

1. Bring water in a sauce pan to boil. Add noodles and stir, then remove them from heat. Allow to stand as noodles soften, then drain.

2. Heat the oil in large-sized pot on med. heat. Cook onion, shallots and garlic until they are softened.

3. Add lemon grass, sugar, chilies, lime zest, fish sauce, vinegar, coconut milk, tomato juice and stock. Bring up to boil on med-high. Add basil and cilantro. Lower heat to med-low. Allow to simmer for about 10 minutes.

4. Remove the basil, garlic and cilantro from the pot. Add mushrooms and tomatoes. Return to simmer. Add lime juice and calamari and season using salt pepper, as desired.

5. Divide the noodles in four bowls. Pour broth into hot pot on table burner. Provide chopsticks or fondue forks so diners can cook their scallops and shrimp, and have dipping sauces on table for their use.

9 – Tofu Mushroom Hot Pot

The spicy, ginger-infused broth that **Makes** this hot pot meal satisfying is the key to why so many people love it. It adds all the extra flavors you'll need to enjoy tofu as a main dish ingredient.

Makes 6 Servings

Cooking + Prep Time: 30 minutes

Ingredients:

- ½ cup of cilantro, chopped
- 8 oz. of lo-Mein noodles, fresh
- 4 cups of Bok choy greens, sliced thinly
- ¼ cup of soy sauce, reduced sodium
- 4 cups of broth, vegetable
- 1 tbsp. of sugar, brown
- 4 oz. of stemmed, sliced mushrooms, shiitake
- 6 minced garlic cloves
- 2 tbsp. of ginger, fresh, grated
- 2 tsp. of oil, canola
- 14 oz. of tofu, firm
- Dipping sauces, your choice – see recipe 1

Instructions:

1. Drain tofu and rinse. Cut into cubes of about 1" in size.

2. Heat oil in pot on med. heat. Add garlic and ginger. Stir while cooking until they are fragrant. Add the mushrooms. Cook until a bit soft.

3. Stir in soy sauce, broth and sugar. Add the Bok choy. Cover. Simmer 'til Bok choy wilts. Raise heat up to med-

high. Add noodles. Cover. Cook until the noodles become tender. Remove from heat. Stir cilantro in.

4. Pour boiling broth into hot pot on table with a burner under it. Allow diners to use their own chopsticks to cook their tofu chunks in the hot broth.

10 – Beef Mince Hot Pot

Straight from Britain, we have a beef mince hot pot recipe. It's satisfying, cheap and tasty. You can add additional vegetables like green beans or broccoli, if you like.

Makes 3 Servings

Cooking + Prep Time: 25 minutes

Ingredients:

- 8 potatoes
- Udon noodles, 1 pkg.
- 10 ounces of water, boiling
- 2-3 tbsp. of gravy granules, beef
- 14 oz. of beef mince
- 1 chopped onion
- 6 sliced mushrooms
- 1 handful of peas, frozen
- 1 chopped carrot
- A drizzle of oil, olive

Instructions:

1. Warm a bit of oil in fry pan on med. heat. Add beef mince. Break apart while browning until the meat is not pink any longer. Add onion, mushrooms, peas and carrots. Stir while cooking for about five minutes.

2. Sprinkle gravy granules into pan. Pour into boiling water in pot. Bring to simmer while you stir it occasionally.

3. Bring sauce pan of water to boil. Add potatoes. Cook until they are tender, or about 10 minutes. Drain. Allow to cool and then slice them.

4. Top mince with potato slices and drizzle using olive oil. Cook mixture in pot for about 20 minutes.

5. Cook noodles according to package instructions. Divide among individual bowls. Serve hot.

11 – Vietnamese Hot Pot

The Vietnamese have a well-learned knack for preparing memorable hot pot dinners. They understand that if you add more **Ingredients** and simmer them longer, your hot pot meal will be more aromatic and tasty.

Makes 5-7 Servings

Cooking + Prep Time: 2 hours and 15 minutes

Ingredients:

For stock

- 1 to 2 sliced celeriac, whole
- 2 to 3 sliced carrots
- 3 pounds of chicken
- 4 ¼ quarts of filtered water
- 2 diced onions
- 2 or 3 bay leaves
- 12 peppercorns
- 1 bunch parsley
- Lime leaves, crushed lime, salt and pepper

For hot pot

- 1 tbsp. of fish sauce
- 1 or 2 chilies, fresh
- 2 or 3 diced bulbs, ginger
- 3 to 4 cloves of garlic
- 1 tbsp. of tamarind paste
- 2 or 3 broken-up stems of lemon grass

To serve

- Favorite seafood or meat
- Dipping sauces, your choice – see recipe 1

Instructions:

1. For stock, add a bit of oil and fry onion and chicken until stock is aromatic. Add other **Ingredients**. Simmer for three hours or more on med-low.

2. For hot pot, fry brown sugar, fish sauce, chilies, tamarind paste, lemon grass, ginger and garlic cloves. When aromatic and hot, add chicken stock and simmer for 30 minutes or so.

3. When broth in hot pot is done simmering, remove the spices. Move the broth to table. Place hot pot on burner. Bring to boil one time before reducing the heat.

4. Add plates of hot pot **Ingredients**. Your diners can use small sieves (found in Asian markets) to strain out their desired food chunks.

12 – Onion Potato Hot Pot

What to do when you walk in the door and realize there are no meal-ready foods in the fridge or the pantry? If you want something to warm you up, just grab a few onions and potatoes. It's simple to make and the family will enjoy really sharing a meal.

Makes 3-4 Servings

Cooking + Prep Time: 1 1/2 hours

Ingredients:

- 6 rashers of bacon
- 32 ounces of reduced salt stock, chicken or vegetable
- 3 sliced onions, medium
- 2 ¼ pounds of sliced potatoes
- 1 pinch of black pepper, ground

Instructions:

1. Preheat oven to 375F.

2. Arrange one layer of potato slices and then one layer of sliced onions in a baking dish. Continue to alternate layers. Season layers with pepper. The top layer should be one of potatoes.

3. Pour in stock. Bake in oven for an hour. Arrange bacon on top. Cook for 15 more minutes. Serve in individual bowls.

13 – Sausage Lentil Hot Pot

This warming hot pot dish is ideal for cold fall and winter nights. It's an easy soup that is such a meal in one bowl. Just toss the veggies in the pot to get them ready, and enjoy chatting with your guests as you all cook your own sausage.

Makes 4 Servings

Cooking + Prep Time: 1 hour 35 minutes

Ingredients:

- 1 pound of sausages, pork
- 67 oz. of stock, chicken
- 1 chopped onion
- 1 tbsp. of oil, olive
- 3 ounces of barley, pearl
- 6 ounces of lentils, green
- 9 ounces of peeled, chopped potatoes
- 5 1/3 oz. of washed, chopped leeks
- 3 ½ oz. of peeled, chopped parsnips
- 9 oz. of washed, chopped carrots

Instructions:

1. Preheat oven to 350F.

2. Heat olive oil and sausages in large casserole dish until they are brown. Remove sausages and set them aside.

3. Add onion. Fry until it is soft. Add the rest of the veggies to casserole dish. Stir to combine. Add 67 oz. of stock, lentils and barley. Cook on high for five minutes.

4. Transfer pan to oven. Cook for 60 minutes more.

5. Cut sausages into small bite-sized pieces.

6. Pour casserole bowl stock into hot pot on table. Give diners chopsticks to reheat the sausages.

14 – Pumpkin Udon Hot Pot

This pumpkin and noodle hot pot is an excellent way to become accustomed to the kabocha pumpkin. It breaks down a bit as it cooks, which thickens and enriches the soup. It's a wonderful vegetarian meal, both satisfying and sweet.

Makes 4 Servings

Cooking + Prep Time: 5 hours and 45 minutes including 5 hours standing time

Ingredients:

- 1 lb. of Udon noodles, precooked, frozen
- 3 ½ oz. of trimmed, separated mushrooms
- 4 oz. of sliced cabbage, Napa
- 1 medium peeled, halved, sliced carrot
- 3 small peeled, quartered taro roots
- 4 oz. of peeled, halved, sliced daikon
- ½ de-seeded and cut kabocha pumpkin
- 2 x 6" pieces of kombu (kelp)
- ½ cup of soy sauce, low sodium
- ½ cup of mirin
- 8 pcs. of shiitake mushrooms, dried

Instructions:

1. Place the mushrooms in large sized bowl. Add five cups of filtered water. Cover. Allow to sit for five hours at room temperature.

2. Strain the liquid into another large bowl. Reserve mushrooms and liquid. Trim and discard the stems. Add mirin and soy sauce to the bowl. Set it aside.

3. Place the kombu in cast iron pot. Top with the mushrooms, cabbage, carrot, taro, daikon and pumpkin. Pour in the mushroom liquid, too.

4. Cover the pot. Bring to boil on high heat. Lower heat to med. Simmer for about 10 minutes. Remove cover. Add the noodles. Simmer until the noodles become tender. Serve in individual bowls.

15 – Green Bean Ginger Hot Pot

I always enjoy making hot pot dinners in the fall and winter months. This hot pot dish is like a chunky soup that we make ourselves. It's a tasty way to fill up, and healthy, too.

Makes 4 Servings

Cooking + Prep Time: 40 minutes

Ingredients:

- 8 oz. of trimmed and sliced green beans
- 4 sliced carrots

- 4 sliced green onions, white and green parts
- 1 tsp. of chili sauce, as desired
- 1 tbsp. of oil, olive
- 1 x 3.75-oz. package of rice noodles, thin
- 2 tbsp. of ginger, grated
- 2/3 cup of soy sauce, low-sodium
- 6 cups of broth, chicken or vegetable, low sodium
- 8 oz. of mushrooms with caps sliced and stems removed

Instructions:

1. Prepare noodles using directions on package. Drain. Cut into three-inch pieces.

2. Heat oil in sauce pan on med-high heat. Add mushrooms. Stir occasionally while cooking for about two minutes.

3. Add chili sauce, ginger, soy sauce and broth. Combine well and bring to boil.

4. Add green beans, scallions and carrots. Simmer about five to six minutes 'til veggies become tender.

5. Divide noodles into individual bowls. Allow diners to ladle soup on top.

16 – Lancashire Potato Hot Pot

This hot pot recipe originated in Lancashire, England. It features lamb and potatoes baked in a large pot over low heat. It's a slow-cooked, wonderful classic when you're in one of those meat and potato moods.

Makes 4 Servings

Cooking + Prep Time: 90 minutes

Ingredients:

- 1 pound of sliced potatoes
- 1 sprig of thyme, fresh
- 20 ounces of hot lamb stock
- 2 chunk-cut carrots, large
- 1 sliced onion, yellow
- 4 x 4 ½ ounce lamb steaks, boneless, sliced thinly
- 2 tbsp. of oil, olive
- 2 tbsp. of flour, all-purpose
- ¾ ounce of melted butter
- 1 broken bay leaf
- 2 tsp. of Worcestershire sauce
- Dipping sauces, your choice – see recipe 1

Instructions:

1. Heat oil in large pan on med. heat. Add carrots and onions. Cook and stir occasionally for three to four minutes. They should brown lightly.

2. Stir in stock and bring to simmer. Stir in herbs and Worcestershire sauce. Season. Remove from heat.

3. Add potato slices to the pan. Heat until they are soft and tender.

4. Pour stock and veggies into hot pot with heat source under it at dining table.

5. Have diners use chopsticks to dip the lamb into the boiling stock to cook. Have dressings available

– see recipe 1.

17 – Spicy Lo Mein Tofu Hot Pot

This filling hot pot meal will warm you up on any chilly evening. The tofu pulls in the flavors from the spicy, fragrant broth, which Makes it so tantalizing. You can find the Lo Mein noodles in refrigerated sections of supermarkets.

Makes 6 Servings

Cooking + Prep Time: 35 minutes

Ingredients:

- 2 tbsp. of ginger, grated
- 4 oz. of stemmed, sliced mushrooms, shiitake
- ¼ cup of soy sauce, reduced sodium
- 4 cups of broth, vegetable or chicken, reduced sodium
- 2 tsp. of oil, canola
- 4 cups of Bok choy greens, sliced thinly
- 14 oz. of tofu, firm
- 1 tbsp. of sugar, brown
- 6 minced garlic cloves
- ½ cup of cilantro, chopped
- 8 oz. of Lo Mein noodles
- For dipping: chili-Garlic Sauce

Instructions:

1. Drain, rinse and dry tofu. Cut into one-inch cubes.

2. Heat the oil in Dutch oven on med. heat. Add garlic and ginger. Stir and cook until fragrant. Add the mushrooms. Cook until they are a bit soft.

3. Stir in soy sauce, broth and sugar. Cover. Bring to boil.

4. Add Bok choy. Simmer until the greens wilt. Raise heat back to high. Add noodles. Cook until they are tender. Remove from heat. Add cilantro.

5. Pour broth into hot pot on serving table. Give diners chopsticks to use in cooking their cubes of tofu. Have dipping sauce on table.

18 – Pork Mushroom Hot Pot

This mushroom and pork hot pot recipe is a winner in the winter. You can warm yourself up, along with your family and any lucky guests you invite over. It's healthy and filling, and all you need to do is drop the Ingredients in the hot pot.

Makes 3-5 Servings

Cooking + Prep Time: 50 minutes

Ingredients:

- 3 sliced green onions
- ¾ pounds of pork tenderloin, sliced thinly

- 4 oz. of mushrooms
- 1 x 2" piece of sliced ginger
- 5 smashed cloves of garlic, medium
- 6 tbsp. of soy sauce, reduced sodium
- ¼ cup of sherry
- 6 cups of chicken broth, low-sodium
- Dipping sauces, your choice – see recipe 1

Instructions:

1. Combine the broth with mushroom stems, ginger, garlic, soy sauce and sherry. Bring to boil on med-high and reduce to low, to simmer. This allows the broth to become infused with the flavors, and takes about a half-hour.

2. Strain the broth. Return to the pot on high heat. Bring to boil. Lower heat to low and add mushrooms. Cook until they are softened.

3. Pour boiling broth into hot pot. Place on table. Give diners fondue forks or chopsticks to use in dipping their pork in the broth to cook. Have dipping sauces available.

19 – Thai Chicken Hot Pot

Thai hot pot is a favorite recipe at noodle restaurants. It is so filling and wonderfully flavorful. The chicken-based stock is infused with veggie flavors that come through in the chicken as it is dipped and cooked.

Makes 6 Servings

Cooking + Prep Time: 1 hour

Ingredients:

- 1 x 13 ½ oz. can of coconut milk, light
- 1 cup of chicken broth, low sodium
- ¾ cup of rice, jasmine
- 1 thinly sliced bell pepper, red
- 2 tbsp. of lime juice
- 1 tsp. of cayenne pepper
- 1 tbsp. of low sodium soy sauce
- 1 pound of boneless, skinless chicken breasts, sliced thinly
- 1 tsp. of oil, canola
- ¼ cup of chopped cilantro
- ½ cup of chopped green onions
- Dipping sauces, your choice – see recipe 1

Instructions:

1. Heat the oil in large pan on med. heat. Add lime juice, soy sauce and cayenne pepper. Cook for two minutes and remove to bowl.

2. In the same pan, stir and cook the bell peppers for four to five minutes. Add the rice. Cook for three more minutes.

3. Add coconut milk and stock. Bring to simmer. Cover. Reduce the heat to med-low. Cook while covered for 20 minutes.

4. Remove from heat. Allow to stand covered for a few minutes. Pour into hot pot and place the pot on heat unit on table. Diners will use chopsticks to cook their chicken slices. Have dipping sauces handy, too.

20 – Chinese Mung Bean Hot Pot

This wonderful Chinese hot pot dish is filled with chicken, vegetables and noodles. It's nice to find a meal that is user-friendly, healthy and comforting.

Makes 6 Servings

Cooking + Prep Time: 35 minutes

Ingredients:

- 4 Bok choy, baby

- 8 oz. of mushrooms
- 1 ½ cups of sprouts, mung bean
- 1 bunch scallions
- 5 oz. of rice noodles
- 1-lb. of chicken thighs, boneless, sliced thinly
- 3 to 5 cracked cloves of garlic
- 6 cups of filtered water
- 6 cups of stock, chicken, low sodium
- 3 to 5 slices of ginger, fresh
- 1 ½ tbsp. of oil, sesame
- 1/3 cup of soy sauce
- ½ cup of vinegar, rice

Instructions:

1. Bring chicken stock, garlic, ginger, sesame oil, soy sauce, vinegar and water to boil in large sized pot. Add noodles. Stir. Cover. Remove from heat.

2. Chop veggies and put them in small serving bowls. When you're ready to serve, allow each diner to fill his bowl with veggies and some chili sauce. Ladle boiling soup over veggies and allow the veggies to cook for five minutes.

21 – Bavarian Hot Pot

Layering vegetables and meats is popular in Bavarian dishes. But some German recipes take a long time to make, whereas this one is quick. Most of the liquids will cook away, so you're left with a wonderful mixture of sausage and veggies.

Makes 5-6 Servings

Cooking + Prep Time: 40 minutes

Ingredients:

- ¾ lb. of thinly sliced kielbasa
- 3 cups of broth, beef
- 2 cups of fresh peas, shelled
- 1 lb. of peeled cubed potatoes
- 6 oz. of snapped green beans
- 2 peeled sliced carrots
- 1 lb. of cored sliced cabbage
- 2 tbsp. of parsley, chopped
- 1 tsp. of crumbled leaf marjoram, dried
- 1 tsp. of caraway seeds
- 1/8 tsp. of nutmeg, ground
- 1/8 tsp. of black pepper, ground
- ½ tsp. of salt
- Dipping sauces, your choice – see recipe 1

Instructions:

1. Place broth, nutmeg, salt pepper, peas, potatoes, beans, carrots and cabbage in a large pot. Set on med. heat and bring to boil.

2. Adjust heat level so broth is gently bubbling. Cover. Do not stir while cooking for about 20 minutes. Add marjoram and caraway seeds. Lightly toss and mix.

3. Cover again. Simmer for about 10 minutes. Add the parsley. Toss lightly. Serve in bowls with chunks of bread and kielbasa to cook in the broth. Offer dipping sauce, as well.

22 – Asian Beef Mushroom Hot Pot

What's better than a tasty dinner? A tasty dinner shared with friends. This is a nutritious dish, too. You'll enjoy the vegetables, meat, rice and noodles, all in one dish. Everyone can cook the meats just how they like them.

Makes 3-4 Servings

Cooking + Prep Time: 40 minutes

Ingredients:

- 8 ounces of mushrooms
- 1 tbsp. of oil, olive
- 3 ¾ oz. rice noodles, thin

- 1 lb. of lean beef, thinly sliced
- 6 cups of broth, vegetable
- 2 tbsp. of ginger, grated
- ½ cup of soy sauce, low sodium
- 8 oz. of trimmed, sliced green beans
- 4 thinly sliced carrots
- 4 sliced green onions
- Chili sauce for dipping

Instructions:

1. Prepare noodles using directions on the package. Drain. Cut into lengths of three inches.

2. Heat oil in sauce pan on med-high. Add mushrooms. Stir occasionally while cooking for about two minutes.

3. Add ginger, soy sauce and broth. Combine and bring to boil.

4. Add green beans, green onions and carrots. Simmer until veggies are becoming tender.

5. Have diners used chopsticks to cook sliced beef in hot pot.

6. Divide noodles in individual bowls. Ladle some leftover soup over tops of noodles.

23 – Korean Dumpling Hot Pot

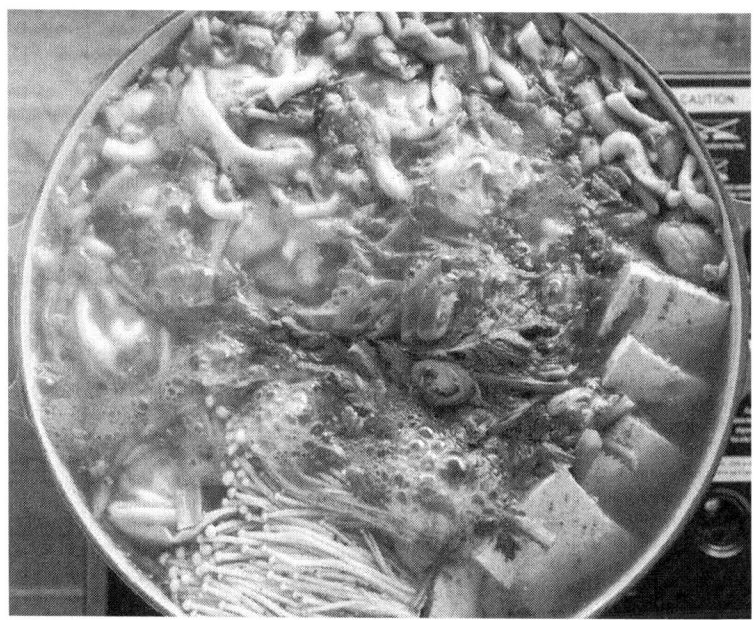

This is much like typical Korean fare, loaded with green veggies, mushrooms, tofu and kimchi. But the highlight of the dish here is the dumplings. They are large dumplings, too, so the dish is quite filling.

Makes 4 Servings

Cooking + Prep Time: 25 minutes

Ingredients:

- 4 cups of Korean soup or vegetable stock
- 1 ½ oz. of sliced onions
- ¾ oz. of sliced green onions
- 7 oz. of mushrooms, your choice
- 10 ½ oz. of sliced kimchi
- 7 oz. of enoki mushrooms with stems removed
- 10 ½ oz. of sliced tofu, firm, no more than ½ inches thick
- 1 ¼ lbs. of dumplings, your choice
- For dipping: Korean chili sauce, bottled

Instructions:

1. Place the Ingredients as they are prepared into a large pot. Boil on med-high until you have a rapid boil. Reduce heat to med-low.

2. Begin serving as your individual Ingredients are ready. Allow diners to cook vegetables and tofu in the hot pot at the table.

24 – Miso Noodle Hot Pot

This comforting, warm dish includes all kinds of Ingredients that warm you up on cold winter or fall evenings. The thinly sliced pork, squash and tofu make a wonderful combination.

Makes 4 Servings

Cooking + Prep Time: 1/2 hour

Ingredients:

- ½ pound of thinly sliced pork
- 4 pcs. of aburaage (pouches of tofu)

- 1 pound of Udon noodles
- ½ of 1 kabocha squash
- 4 sliced green onions
- 4 cabbage leaves, Napa
- 1/3 cup of miso
- 1 ½ tsp. of dashi
- 6 cups of filtered water
- Dipping sauces, your choice – see recipe 1

Instructions:

1. Scoop seeds from squash. Cut squash into wedges, then into ¼" slices.

2. Bring large sized pot of filtered water to boil. Add udon noodles. Cook for two to three minutes. Drain.

3. In smaller pot of water, also boiling, blanch tofu pouches. Slice into strips.

4. In earthen pot, pour water. Bring to boil. Add the dashi.

5. Combine miso and stock in medium bowl. Whisk until miso dissolves. Set the bowl aside.

6. Add squash to pot. Allow to simmer for about five minutes. Add tofu pouches and cabbage. Add udon noodles and cook for two more minutes. Pour miso and dashi stock back into the earthen pot. Stir and mix well, then add the green onions.

7. Pour stock and soup into hot pot and place on table with burner. Diners can use chopsticks or fondue forks to cook the sliced pork and dip it.

25 – Mongolian Chinese Hot Pot

Hot pot meals are so interactive, and that's what keeps people making them, and inviting friends over to share them. This type of meal will likely become a tradition in your family.

Makes 4 Servings

Cooking + Prep Time: 25 minutes

Ingredients:

- 8 cups of broth, chicken
- 1 block of tofu, firm
- 1 lb. of Bok choy
- 4 oz. of noodles
- 1 lb. lamb, sliced thinly
- For dipping: bottled sesame dipping sauce

Instructions:

1. Pour bottled sesame dipping sauce into individual bowls.

2. Place noodles and Bok choy in separate bowls, and lamb on plate. Place these around your hot pot location on table.

3. Heat the broth in the hot pot.

4. For serving, each diner will dip lamb in the broth until it is cooked (it only takes a few seconds). They will remove it from hot pot to their individual sauce bowl to eat.

5. After meat is gone, add the Bok choy, tofu and noodles to hot pot. Cook for several minutes. Divide among your guests' bowls. Add more sauce if they prefer.

26 – Sukiyaki Vegan Hot Pot

The main taste-maker in sukiyaki is the broth that is used to marinate the noodles and veggies. And you can include all these elements and more in a hot pot recipe that has a taste reminiscent of traditional sukiyaki. Plus, you'll be sharing it with friends.

Makes 2-4 Servings

Cooking + Prep Time: 20 minutes

Ingredients:

- Oil for sautéing vegetables
- 1 x 14-oz. pkg. of tofu, extra firm
- 1 cup of sliced green onions
- 1 cup of carrots, sliced
- 1 cup of broccoli
- 2 cups of shiitake mushrooms, sliced, de-stemmed
- 2 cups of Napa cabbage, chopped
- 4 cups of filtered water
- 2 cups of Bok choy, chopped
- 8 oz. of noodles
- 3 tbsp. of sugar, granulated
- ½ cup of sake
- ¾ cup of mirin
- Dipping sauces, your choice – see recipe 1

Instructions:

1. Soak noodles using hot water to soften them. Drain.

2. Wash chop tofu and vegetables.

3. In large pot, sauté mushrooms and green onions with a bit of oil until they have browned slightly. Set aside.

4. Add mirin, water, sugar and sake to pot. Simmer 'til sugar has dissolved. Add carrots and broccoli. Simmer for several more minutes. Add cabbage and Bok choy. Simmer again for two or three minutes.

5. Reduce heat down to low. Add noodles, green onions and mushrooms. Allow a few more minutes on heat so everything is cooked.

6. Pour into hot pot and place on dining table. Diners will use chopsticks or fondue forks to cook the tofu in the hot broth.

27 – Pork Ribs Hot Pot

This recipe is proof that you can use a hot pot to cook all kinds of foods. The broth will make the pork so tender that it almost melts in your mouth. The other Ingredients and veggies add to the full-bodied taste that Makes this dish a favorite.

Makes 4-6 Servings

Cooking + Prep Time: 20 minutes

Ingredients:

- 1 ½ pounds of pork rib meat, sliced very thinly
- 4 or 5 ginger slices
- 1 tsp. of ketchup
- ½ cup of water, filtered
- 1 tsp. of soy sauce, light
- 2 ½ tbsp. of sugar, granulated
- 5 tbsp. of vinegar
- Dipping sauces, your choice – see recipe 1

Instructions:

1. Heat a large pot. Add oil and use to sauté the ginger slices. Pour in the seasoning and water. Bring the Ingredients to boil. Allow to thicken and stir in ketchup.

2. Pour broth into hot pot on table. Diners will use chopsticks to dip pork slices in the hot broth. Set out dipping sauces, too.

28 – Vegetable Beef Japanese Hot Pot

This dish is healthy, filling and comforting. You can use any of a variety of noodle types, including low calorie and low carb options. The broth is sweet and savory, and the tofu and veggies offer a treat for chilly evenings.

Makes 4 Servings

Cooking + Prep Time: 50 minutes

Ingredients:

- ¼ cup of sake or mirin
- ¼ cup of soy sauce
- ½ cup of dashi or chicken stock
- 4 ½ ounces of firm tofu, broiled, cubed
- 2 ½ chopped scallions, green and white parts
- 1 sliced celery stalk
- 1 sliced carrot, medium
- ½ cup of mushrooms, fresh
- ½ cup of sliced onion, yellow
- ½ pound of beef, well-marbled, sliced thinly
- 1 tbsp. of oil, vegetable, + extra if needed
- Boiling water
- 2 ounces of noodles, shirataki

Instructions:

1. Mix sake or mirin, soy sauce and chicken stock in medium bowl. Adjust if needed and set the bowl aside.

2. Soak noodles in oven-safe bowl for a minute or so in boiling hot water. Drain in colander and then rinse using cold water. Cut in half.

3. In medium hot pot, heat 1 tbsp. of oil on high until it starts shimmering. Add celery, carrots, mushrooms and onion. Cook until barely tender. Add scallions. Stir until they look a brighter green in color.

4. Transfer to hot pot on dining table. Have your guests dip slices of beef and tofu in the hot pot and dip in the sauces provided.

29 – Spicy Whitefish Hot Pot

Even though there are Chinese restaurants all over the world, you won't find this dish very often. The whitefish fillets are served in boiling broth that gives the dish so much taste. You'll love it from the first bite.

Makes 4 Servings

Cooking + Prep Time: 40 minutes

Ingredients:

- 1 pound of thinly sliced fillets, whitefish
- 1 cup of fish stock
- 2 cups of tomato puree
- ½ tsp. of paprika
- 1 tsp. of drained capers
- 2 ½ ounce of olives, green
- 1 chopped Thai chili
- 1 minced garlic clove
- 1 sliced onion
- 1 tbsp. of oil, olive
- Dipping sauces, your choice – see recipe 1

Instructions:

1. Heat the oil in a large pot on high heat. Sauté chili, onion and garlic for two to three minutes. Add paprika, stock and tomato puree. Bring to boil. Reduce to med-low. Add capers and olives.

2. Diners use chopsticks to dip fish into hot pot to cook it, then dip in sauces.

30 – Thai Curry Coconut Hot Pot

Thai curry hot pots are super easy to make, and you can customize them with any favorite veggies you want to use. It can be served as a vegan and gluten-free dish, and it's perfect for inviting friends over to share.

Makes 7-9 Servings

Cooking + Prep Time: 45 minutes

Ingredients:

- ½ head of broccoli, florets only
- 1-pound of thinly sliced beef
- 4 to 6 tbsp. of red curry paste
- 3 x 15-oz. cans of coconut milk
- 8 cups of vegetable stock
- 1" of ginger, sliced
- 5 minced garlic cloves
- 1 tbsp. of oil, olive
- Dipping sauces, your choice – see recipe 1

Instructions:

1. Heat oil in large pot. Add ginger and garlic. Sauté for a couple minutes. Add coconut milk and veggie stock. Stir and combine well.

2. Continue to cook until broth is almost at a simmer. Add curry paste and whisk until it dissolves. Cover. Simmer for about five minutes. Remove slices of ginger.

3. Pour soup into hot pot on table. Have meat and broccoli dippers handy so that they can be cooked in hot soup. Diners can use their choice of dipping sauces.

Conclusion

This hot pot cookbook has shown you…

How to use different **Ingredients** to affect sweet and spicy tastes in hot pot dishes you have heard of, and some that may be new to you.

So, what can you do now?

You can think of hot pot cooking as Asian fondues, where everybody at the communal table gets to cook their own food in a simmering pot of broth. It's a wonderful time to share with your friends, as you all enjoy a tasty and filling meal.

Have fun experimenting! Enjoy the results!

Made in the USA
Lexington, KY
24 November 2018